TARGETING U.S. TECHNOLOGIES:

"A Trend Analysis of Reporting from Defense Industry"

2010

TABLE OF CONTENTS

TABLES AND FIGURES

In the interests of readability and comprehension, the editors have deferred the conventional stylistic use of repeated acronyms in favor of a full exposition of terms as they are first used within each section.

TARGETING U.S. TECHNOLOGIES:
A TREND ANALYSIS OF REPORTING FROM DEFENSE INDUSTRY

As noted in the Office of the National Counterintelligence Executive's "Annual Report to Congress on Foreign Economic Collection and Industrial Espionage," the threat to the United States from foreign economic intelligence collection and industrial espionage has continued unabated and foreign entities continue to try to illegally acquire U.S. technology, trade secrets, and proprietary information.

The mission of the Defense Security Service (DSS) is to support national security and the warfighter, secure the nation's technological base, and oversee the protection of both U.S. and foreign classified nformation in the hands of industry. This report is based on information obtained from DSS outreach and partnerships with stakeholders and customers, and includes the agency's analysis of suspicious contact reports received from cleared industry.

Without a strong partnership with cleared industry to identify and report these attempted collection efforts, this report would not be possible. Nor would it be possible for our partners in law enforcement (the Federal Bureau of Investigation, Department of Homeland Security, and others) to carry out their responsibilities to neutralize and counter the efforts of illicit actors.

As outlined in the National Industrial Security Program Operating Manual, cleared contractor employees inform DSS of suspicious contacts and potential collection attempts. DSS evaluates these reports and refers significant matters to the larger law enforcement communities. It is imperative that our partnership with industry continues to result in timely reporting of improper foreign collection attempts. It is only by working together that we can ensure the continued technological advantage this country has benefited from over the past decades.

Each report the agency receives makes a difference. In fiscal year 2009 (FY09), industry reporting enabled federal investigative or intelligence agencies to initiate close to 50 cases. DSS categorizes these cases of a known or suspected collector attempting to acquire cleared industry information or technology as unlawful penetrations of the cleared industrial base. The overarching goal of the DSS Counterintelligence Directorate is to identify, and ultimately stop, unlawful penetrators. Thanks to reports received from industry in FY09, the country's technological edge was better safeguarded and our national interests were more protected.

The information in this publication will assist you in understanding the nature of the threats that this country faces and will help you to identify and recognize the techniques foreign collectors employ in their efforts to improperly acquire U.S. technologies.

Your success impacts not only our national security, but the future and security of your companies as well. Your continued vigilance constitutes the first line of defense against those who would do us harm. Do not allow your guard to drop

BARRY E. STERLING
Acting Director
Defense Security Service

Department of Defense (DoD) Instruction 5200.39, dated July 16, 2008, requires the Defense Security Service (DSS) to publish a classified report, along with an unclassified companion report, detailing suspicious activities occurring within the cleared contractor community. Accordingly, this report provides important information regarding foreign threats to cleared personnel, information, and technologies resident in the U.S. cleared defense industrial base.

DSS must provide these reports to the DoD Counterintelligence (CI) community, national entities, and the cleared contractor community to assist in general threat awareness, identify specific technologies at risk, and aid in the application of appropriate threat countermeasures. DSS receives and analyzes suspicious contact reports (SCRs) from cleared contractors in accordance with reporting requirements as defined in Chapter 1, Section 3 of the National Industrial Security Program Operating Manual, 5220.22-M, dated February 28, 2006. The analysis of these SCRs is the basis for this year's trends report.

The information in this report covers the most prolific foreign collectors targeting the cleared contractor community during fiscal year 2009 (FY09) as compared to the previous year. It includes statistical and trends analysis on foreign collector affiliations, the methods foreign entities used to target the cleared contractor community, and the specific technology sectors that they targeted. Each section also contains an analytical assessment forecasting potential future activities against the cleared contractor community.

This year, information on the attempted acquisition of marine sensors technology within U.S. cleared industry is also included. This specific technology subset was selected based on the reporting DSS received and the assessment that it is a growing interest area for collection. The section provides a definition of marine sensors technology, analysis based on reporting from cleared industry, and the collector methodology.

This report is published as part of DSS' ongoing effort to enhance awareness of foreign entities targeting the U.S. cleared industrial base and to encourage reporting of such incidents as they occur. It is also intended to be a ready reference tool for security professionals in their efforts to detect, deter, mitigate, and neutralize the effects of foreign targeting.

A. SCOPE/METHODOLOGY

DSS provides statistical and trend analysis on the foreign collection threat posed to the cleared contractor community over the past fiscal year as compared to the previous fiscal year.

This report is based primarily on SCRs collected from the cleared contractor community, but also includes references to all-source Intelligence Community (IC) reporting.

While DSS analyzes all SCRs received from industry, only those indicative of potential illicit foreign collection activities in FY09 were used to form the basis of this report. Through analytical processes and application of the DSS foreign intelligence threat assessment methodology, DSS determined over 40 percent of these reports either posed a potential intelligence concern to the cleared contractor community or represented a link to elements DSS determined as hostile to U.S. interests.

DSS analyzes foreign interest in U.S. defense technology in terms of the 20 categories in the Developing Science and Technologies List (DSTL). The DSTL is a compendium of science and technology capabilities being developed worldwide that have the potential to significantly enhance or degrade U.S. military capabilities in the future. It serves as a template for DSS to define categories and subcategories for each technology; identification of said technologies is a critical analytic objective.

As noted, DSS categorizes and culls SCRs to determine a nexus to a foreign-affiliated entity and if they present a threat to the cleared contractor community. DSS analysts scrutinize the SCRs by examining the critical U.S. technologies, the targeting entites, the methods of operation, the relationships to previous reporting from the cleared contractor community, and all-source IC information.

B. EXPLANATION OF ESTIMATIVE LANGUAGE & ANALYTIC CONFIDENCE

DSS adopted the IC estimative language standard for use in the trends analysis reports. The use of synonymous phraseology such as "we judge," "we assess," or "we estimate," and terms such as "likely," or "indicate," represents an effort to convey an analytical assessment or judgment.

These assessments, based on incomplete or at times fragmentary information, are not facts or proof, nor do they represent empirically-based certainty or knowledge. Some analytical judgments are based directly on collected information, others rest on previous judgments, yet both serve as building blocks. In either type of judgment, the agency does not have "evidence" showing something to be a fact or that definitively links two items or issues.

Remote	Unlikely	Even Chance	Probably Likely	Almost Certainly

Intelligence judgments pertaining to "likelihood" are intended to reflect the probability of a development, event, or trend. Assigning precise numerical ratings to such judgments would imply more rigor than the agency intends. The previous chart provides a rough idea of the relationship of terms to each other.

The authors do not intend the term "unlikely" to imply an event will not happen. The report includes "probably" and "likely" to indicate there is a greater than even chance. It includes words such as "we cannot dismiss," "we cannot rule out," and "we cannot discount" to reflect unlikely- or even remote- events whose consequences are such that it warrants mentioning.

Words such as "may" and "suggest" are used to reflect situations in which DSS is unable to assess the likelihood generally because relevant information is nonexistent, sketchy, or fragmented.

In addition to using words within a judgment to convey degrees of likelihood, DSS also ascribes analytic confidence levels based on the scope and quality of information supporting DSS judgments.

- **High Confidence:** Judgments are based on high-quality information, or the nature of the issue makes it possible to render a solid judgment.

- **Moderate Confidence:** Information can be interpreted in various ways, DSS has alternative views, or the

information is credible and plausible but not corroborated sufficiently to warrant a higher level of confidence.

- **Low Confidence:** Information is scant, questionable, or highly fragmented, making solid analytic inferences difficult, or that DSS has significant concerns or problems with the sources.

EXECUTIVE SUMMARY

The Defense Security Service (DSS) proudly presents its 12th annual "Targeting U.S. Technologies" report in response to cleared industry's desire for analysis concerning the foreign collection threat against U.S. technologies resident in cleared industry. Through analyzing reports concerning cleared industry's contacts with foreign entities, DSS is uniquely positioned to provide an essential and valuable perspective on how foreign collectors are attempting to acquire access to sensitive or classified Department of Defense (DoD) information and technologies resident in cleared industry.

These reports from industry, known as suspicious contact reports (SCRs), illustrate the methods foreign collectors use to illicitly obtain information, the common affiliations or surrogates they use to avoid raising suspicion, and foreign collection requirements and targeting. Our key findings are based on DSS analysis of fiscal year 2009 (FY09) data compared to the previous year's reporting.

A. KEY FINDINGS

- For the past decade, entities from the East Asian and the Pacific region have been, and continue to be, the most active collectors targeting cleared industry. East Asian and Pacific collectors continued to aggressively target cleared industry for classified and restricted technology and information. This pervasive threat exploits relationships with industry, circumvents export control laws, and boldly uses cyber attacks to target U.S. information resident in cleared industry.

- The use of the commercial sector, with the intent to make contacts more innocuous when targeting industry, continued to dominate more traditional, government-affiliated collection attempts. For the fourth year in a row, commercial entities' contact with cleared industry surged, with these purported private sector entities seeking an unprecedented number of privatized research and development (R&D) ventures with U.S. cleared industry. Analysis suggests that while some of this increase is no doubt a reflection of increased globalization of the marketplace, this likely represents, in part, an apparent shift on the part of foreign governments to mask officially-sponsored collection efforts as seemingly less-alerting inquiries.

- **Exploitation of the Internet to illicitly acquire technology and information, both through direct email requests and also through the medium of cyber operations, continued to dominate industry reporting.** The Internet continued to offer foreign intelligence entities a low-cost, high gain method to target cleared industry for sensitive or classified technology and information. The exponential growth of the Internet allowed for increased connectivity for legitimate global business and also as a means for surreptitious access to cleared contractor facility networks.

- **Marine sensors technology has increased as a priority target.** In FY09, foreign entities increased overt targeting and collection of cleared contractor-developed marine sensors technology and information. Accelerated by increasing maritime trade competitiveness and an aggressive regional marketplace for marine-related technology, foreign entities increased collection of naval R&D initiatives in efforts to modernize naval arsenals and increase maritime-based capabilities.

B. REGIONAL TRENDS

DSS examined SCRs received from cleared industry in FY09 to determine which reports represented matters of confirmed or probable counterintelligence (CI) concern. Where possible, analysts affiliated relevant reports with specific regions of origin, assessing the geographic or ethnic association of the requestor.

The FY09 hierarchy of top regional collectors of origin did not change dramatically in comparison to the previous year's rankings. As has been the case since DSS first began to compile comparative statistics, East Asian and Pacific entities continued to dominate as the most prolific regional collectors of U.S. technology and

FIGURE 1

REGIONAL TRENDS

East Asia
and the Pacific

Near East

South and
Central Asia

Europe
and Eurasia

The regions most frequently affiliated with validated or probable reports of CI concern in FY09 are pictured in descending order above.

information, most likely reflecting the dual imperatives of prominent regional actors to pursue accelerated military modernization efforts and achieve regional dominance.

In a slight change to last year's reporting, South and Central Asian collectors supplanted European and Eurasian entities as the third most prolific requestors of U.S. defense technology and information. European and Eurasian collectors were relegated to placement as the fourth-most prolific collectors, but this decline was more attributable to modest increases in reported collection attempts from South and Central Asian and Near Eastern collectors as opposed to any real decrease in the number of contacts emanating out of Europe and Eurasia.

However, the relative paucity of industry reports related to European and Eurasian collection efforts remains somewhat of a paradox. While U.S. Intelligence Community (IC) assessments continue to document a significant level of foreign success in exploiting U.S.-developed technologies, the lower volume of FY09 industry reporting corresponding to European and Eurasian efforts does not fully correlate to the presumed level of success attributed to individual countries in this region. This analytic disconnect underscores that cleared contractor employees should remain vigilant against this threat and continue to report any improper attempts to collect export-controlled or classified technology and information.

C. COLLECTOR AFFILIATIONS

DSS analyzes each SCR to determine the collector's affiliation and ascertain which foreign entity category is targeting U.S. technology.

Once again, commercial entities were the top collectors of U.S. technology in FY09, representing nearly a third of the contacts with U.S. industry. The emergence of a globally integrated marketplace offers commercial affiliates an efficient and frequently logical avenue of approach to initiate contact with U.S. industry and may represent a conscious effort on the part of foreign governments to mask official interest using commercial surrogates to obtain information.

Collection attempts by unknown affiliates also increased in FY09, primarily attributable to illicit cyber activity affecting defense industry where analysis identified the region of origin but could not specifically attribute end-user affiliation.

FIGURE 2

COLLECTOR AFFILIATIONS

Commercial
Businesses in the commercial and
defense sectors

Government Affiliated
Research institutes, labatories, government-
funded universities, or contractors representing
a government agency

Government
Ministry of Defense, foreign military attachés,
branches of the military

Individual
Persons seeking financial gain, persons avoiding
traditional export procedures, or persons
purportedly seeking academic or
research information

Unknown
Instances when analysis could not directly
attribute the contact to a specific
end-user affiliation

The affiliations above describe a sampling of
the types of collectors in descending order of
occurrence based on FY09 reporting.

D. METHODS OF OPERATION

Once DSS identifies the requestor's
region of origin as well as their
probable affiliation, DSS assesses
the methods of operation (MOs) that
the requestor employs to acquire
information or technology. Our
analysis of these MOs assists cleared
contractor personnel in recognizing
suspicious attempts to acquire
sensitive or classified information and

aids in the application of appropriate
countermeasures to mitigate or
negate their effectiveness.

Utilization of direct requests for
information continued to be, by far,
the most common technique foreign

FIGURE 3

METHODS OF OPERATION

Direct Request
Email requests for information, web-card
purchase requests, price quote requests,
phone calls, or marketing surveys

Foreign Visits and Targeting
Suspicious activity at a
convention, unannounced visit to a cleared
contractor, solicitations to attend a convention,
offers of paid travel to a seminar, targeting
of travelers, questions beyond scope, or overt
search and seizure

Solicitation and
Seeking Employment
Offering technical and business services to
cleared contractors, resumé submissions, or
sales offers

Suspicious Internet Activity
Confirmed intrusion, attempted intrusion,
computer network attack, potential
pre-attack, or spam

Exploitation of Relationships
Establishing a joint venture, official agreements,
document peer reviews, scientific board reviews,
foreign military sales, business arrangements, or
cultural commonality

Other
Methodologies not otherwise captured above

The methods described above exemplify
the most common methods of operation in
descending order of occurrence based on
FY09 reporting.

entities used in attempting to acquire U.S. technology or information.

In FY09, DSS analysis also noted significant increases in the use of the foreign visits and targeting technique, especially targeting public venues where cleared contractor technology was on open display. Industry reporting showed that some nations used surrogates, or front companies, to circumvent U.S. export control laws or perceived trade restrictions in efforts to collect information or technology inconspicuously.

E. TARGETED TECHNOLOGIES

DSS analyzes foreign interest in U.S. cleared industry technology in terms of the 20 categories detailed in the Developing Science and Technologies List. Identifying the technologies suspicious entities are targeting is a critical analytic objective and allows U.S. cleared industry to establish appropriately focused security countermeasures to help mitigate the loss of technology and classified information.

This listing is generally consistent with previous years' assessments. Foreign entities continued to target information systems technology most frequently, primarily focusing on modeling and simulation software for military modernization programs.

The remaining technical categories retained their relative hierarchical positions, but interest in sensors

technology, primarily as they relate to marine sensors and programs, saw the largest increase, owing to growing interest in the acquisition of information and technologies identifiable with sonar buoys, autonomous underwater vehicles, and sensors for the U.S. Navy's Littoral Combat Ship program.

FIGURE 4

TARGETED TECHNOLOGIES

Information Systems

Sensors

Aeronautics

Electronics

Lasers and Optics

Positioning, Navigation, and Time

Marine Systems

Armaments and Energetic Materials

Ground Systems

Materials and Processing

Space Systems

The figure above illustrates the most targeted technologies in descending order of occurrence based on FY09 reporting.

F. SPECIAL FOCUS AREA: MARINE SENSORS TECHNOLOGY

This report contains a section focused on the increasing prominence of marine sensors technology as an emerging collection target. Not only do the world's oceans offer a major thoroughfare for global shipping and economic endeavors, but they also offer a wide platform for naval military modernization, weapons procurement and proliferation. In FY09, industry reporting of foreign contacts indicated increased attempts to acquire marine sensors technology and information.

Foreign targeting of these capabilities was wide-based, but concentrated among actors from East Asia and the Pacific, the Near East, and South and Central Asia. Collectors likely targeted emerging marine technology in efforts to transform their capabilities from brown-water to blue-water. Because the United States is a world leader in naval R&D and naval defense technologies, cleared contractor employees should be aware of this burgeoning threat and continue to take precautions to secure marine systems technologies in their custody.

SPECIAL FOCUS AREA: MARINE SENSORS

SPECIAL FOCUS AREA: MARINE SENSORS

1. OVERVIEW

The ocean covers 71 percent of the earth's surface and is a major conduit for geopolitical objectives, global shipping endeavors, and littoral warfare. However, as it relates to technology, not all naval engagements are fought on or below the seas. Defense Security Service (DSS) analysis of reporting from industry clearly demonstrates that foreign entities, some acting under state sponsorship, consistently target U.S. cleared industry for littoral research and development (R&D) initiatives and naval defense technologies.

These collection efforts are frequently aimed at transforming indigenous naval arsenals from localized, brown-water forces to strategically important regional or international blue-water navies without having to undertake the massive R&D investment generally required for such an effort. In short,

it is often easier for foreign entities to illicitly acquire U.S. marine technology than to develop it indigenously.

Foreign interest in marine-related technologies has risen steadily over the last 30 years and reports received from industry in fiscal year 2009 (FY09) only underscore this trend. Reporting from industry is consistent with U.S. Intelligence Community (IC) assessments that some developing regional powers, representing potentially adversarial interests towards the United States, are targeting marine technologies with the intent of transforming their respective navies into long-range blue-water maritime forces.

Cleared industry reporting in FY09 suggests this targeting trend has not dissipated and will remain a priority collection emphasis in the years

Blue-Water Navy: A maritime force capable of sustained operation across the deep waters of open oceans. A blue-water navy allows a country to project power far from the home country and usually includes one or more aircraft carriers. Smaller blue-water navies are able to dispatch fewer vessels abroad for shorter periods of time.

Brown-Water Navy: A maritime force focused on riverine or coastal operations close to the home land. While such a navy tends to emphasize the defensive, many littoral vessels have strong offensive capabilities.

ahead. This special interest area highlights the growing intensity of foreign efforts to acquire sensitive U.S. naval technologies.

2. TREND ANALYSIS

Analysis of FY09 industry reporting indicated foreign entity collection attempts of marine technologies nearly tripled from the previous year. In particular, the marine sensors sub-category was one of the top targeted technology areas, as evidenced by the three-fold increase in reports. Analysis of this reporting specifically identified entities originating from East Asia and the Pacific and the Near East as being especially aggressive in targeting cutting-edge, marine sensor technologies.

Countries from these regions have actively targeted cleared industry over the past decade, employing a variety of collection techniques to gain restricted or classified technology and information. Common methods of operation (MO) concerning marine-related technologies included asking for information directly through various media like emails and faxes, exploiting face-to-face contacts to request information during foreign visits to cleared contractor facilities, and offering and seeking business relationships or employment opportunities within cleared industry.

2.1 MARINE SENSORS COUNTRIES OF ORIGIN

While marine R&D programs vary regionally, industry reporting indicates all regions in FY09 were active in targeting the full range of technologies appearing on the Developing Science and Technology List (DSTL).

Reporting from industry clearly demonstrates that foreign entities, some acting under state sponsorship, consistently target U.S. cleared industry for littoral research and development (R&D) initiatives and naval defense technologies.

East Asian and Pacific entities were the most prolific collectors, accounting for the largest share of requests for marine-related technologies, including over 40 percent of all reporting related to marine sensors. The need to close technology gaps and naval modernization efforts likely drove this collection focus with the intent to establish blue-water navies capable of autonomous self-sustaining defense, regional dominance, and power projection.

Analyst Comment: Industry reporting is consistent with IC assessments that state illicitly procured, marine sensors technology would likely narrow

FIGURE 5

MARINE SENSORS CASES
Percentages by Region

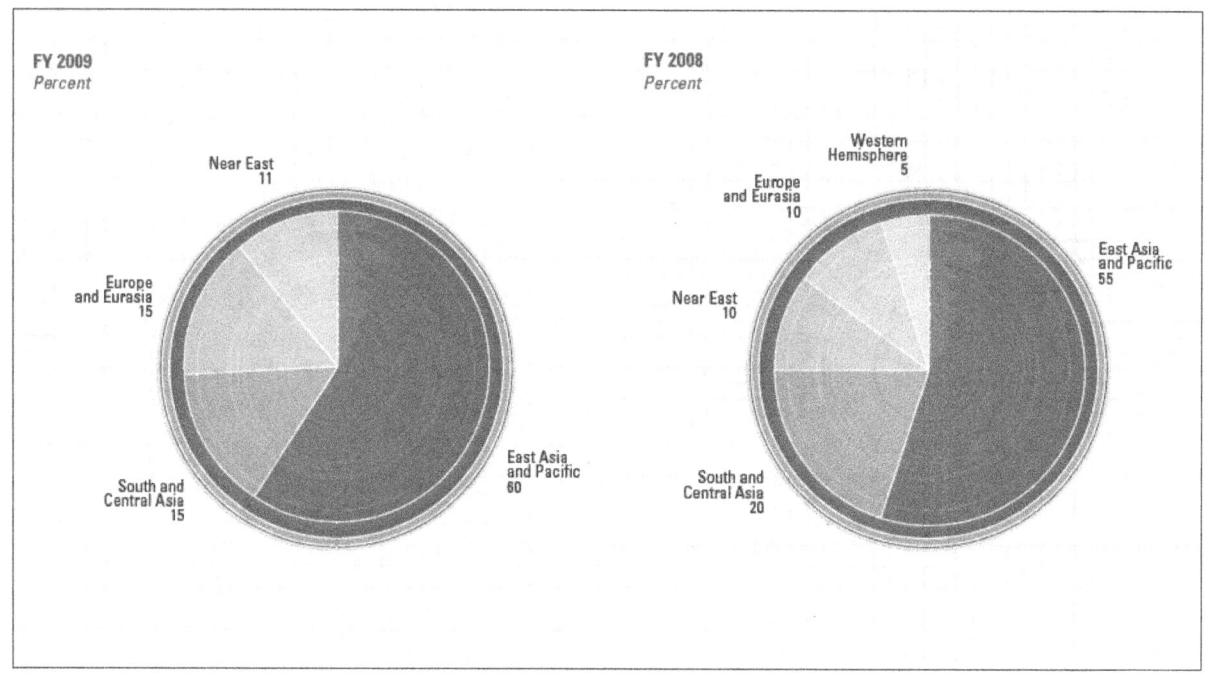

FY 2009
Percent

- Near East 11
- Europe and Eurasia 15
- South and Central Asia 15
- East Asia and Pacific 60

FY 2008
Percent

- Western Hemisphere 5
- Europe and Eurasia 10
- Near East 10
- South and Central Asia 20
- East Asia and Pacific 55

this technological gap and aid naval modernization plans toward blue-water navies. It is almost certain East Asian and Pacific entities will continue to target marine sensors technology as they seek to expand regional dominance and control sea lines of communication. (Confidence Level: High)

The number of entities from the Near East that targeted marine sensors technology in FY09 rose significantly from the previous year,

making the region the second most prolific collector of marine sensors technology. Open source reporting indicates the region's willingness to acquire a wide variety of technologies in order to address technological shortcomings and R&D gaps. IC and industry reporting reveal the region's interest in sophisticated, bottom scanning sonar systems and deep-sea diving bells to address those shortcomings and circumvent U.S. export control laws.

Analyst Comment: Entities from the Near East will likely continue to target cleared industry seeking marine sensors technology beyond the scope of what is available from third party suppliers. Their aim is to strengthen coastal defense strategies and improve their naval asymmetric warfare programs. (Confidence Level: Moderate)

South and Central Asian collectors primarily used the direct request method to target cleared industry and focused their collection efforts on detection and neutralization technologies, like sonar buoys and sea-based radar systems.

Analyst Comment: South and Central Asian collectors will likely continue to pursue advanced marine sensors technology to bolster existing naval capabilities focusing on anti-piracy efforts and countering perceived naval threats from regional adversaries. (Confidence Level: Moderate)

2.2. AFFILIATIONS AND METHODS OF OPERATION

Some marine-related technologies fall into more than one category of technologies listed in the DSTL. For example, an individual technology categorized as marine systems may also be appropriately categorized within the sensors sub-category. Examining this sub-category of FY09 reporting, the foreign interest expressed in marine sensors was particularly dramatic.

COMMONLY TARGETED MARINE SENSORS

FY09 industry reporting indicated sound navigation and ranging, or sonar, technology was the most targeted technology of the marine sensors sub-category. Sonar can be either active or passive and is used for a number of applications.

Active sonar employs acoustic signals to echo range and locate underwater objects. Military uses for active sonar include active anti-ship warfare, weapon homing, torpedo defense, mine warfare, swimmer warfare, deep-sea salvage, and underwater communication and navigation.

Passive sonar detects, classifies, identifies, locates, and tracks acoustically radiating vessels for anti-submarine and anti-surface to ship warfare. Navies covertly deploy passive sonar to locate underwater objects.

Industry reporting documented increased collection activities originating from multiple regions, employing a wide spectrum of techniques to target marine sensors technology.

- **East Asian and Pacific** collectors were the most prolific requestors of marine sensors technology in FY09.

- **Near Eastern** collectors used multiple collector affiliations, at times combined with state-sponsored requests, to circumvent foreign military sales and perceived trade restrictions.

- **South and Central Asian** collectors also used multiple collector affiliations, including state and non-state actors, to seek marine sensors and radars.

- **European and Eurasian** collectors used predominately commercial collectors to mask end-user attribution and seek sensors and underwater surveillance technology.

In FY09, suspicious entities increasingly used surrogate commercial and individual collectors to expand on the information acquired through government collection attempts. The suspicious collector affiliates ranged from scientific universities to advanced technology corporations directly requesting marine sensor technology. These non-traditional collectors used misrepresentations at various levels to circumvent export restrictions and mask true end-user affiliation. Many times, foreign collectors would target specific marine sensors technology employing the full range of government, academic, and commercial affiliates.

2.3. TARGETED TECHNOLOGIES

DSS analysis of FY09 industry reporting suggests discernible hierarchies of interest expressed for specific subsets of marine sensor technology. The list below represents the overall subsets most frequently targeted:

- Active Sonar
- Passive Sonar
- Side-scan Arrays
- Sonar Power Amplifiers
- Electro-optical Sensors
- Transducers and Hydrophones
- Sonar Buoys
- X-band Radar

East Asian and Pacific collectors were interested in all sectors, Near Eastern collectors focused primarily on the first two subsets, and South and Central Asian collectors demonstrated interest in the last two subsets.

3. ANALYTICAL FORECAST

Industry reports of foreign interest in U.S.-developed marine technologies tend to validate IC assessments that regions, leveraging the full collection capabilities of their indigenous intelligence services and cooperating surrogates, are mounting extraordinary efforts to modernize naval capabilities to satisfy both military and economic imperatives.[1]

Marine sensors are essential to this objective and provide critical, dual-use applications that sustain economic, political, and military interests. In the near future, foreign collectors are highly likely to increase their efforts to acquire marine sensors technology to enhance maritime capabilities, whether for economic advancement or military advantage, against perceived competitors or potential adversaries.

It is highly likely that foreign collectors will increasingly target cleared industry engaged in marine-related contracts, especially those that work on marine sensor technologies, to bolster their growing need for self-sufficient, long-range maritime forces. (Confidence Level: High)

CASE STUDY

In FY09, a foreign delegation representing various state-sponsored academic institutions located in the East Asian and Pacific region visited a cleared contractor facility. Immediately prior to the visit, the delegation attempted a suspicious, last-minute switch of pre-approved personnel to participate in the visit. The delegation attempted to substitute two representatives who, the previous year, had visited another cleared contractor facility engaged in similar research.

DSS research revealed that during the previous visit, the two proposed substitutes had attempted to collect controlled, autonomous underwater vehicle navigation algorithms and had tried to purchase side-scan sonar technologies well outside the scope of their visit.

Analyst Comment: This collection attempt underscores the tenacity of foreign collectors to target and obtain U.S.-controlled technologies. The foreign visit MO of changing last minute travel plans and adding unannounced persons to the visiting party is a common intelligence collection technique and is likely representative of a focused collection priority on marine sensors technology. (Confidence Level: High)

EAST ASIA
AND THE PACIFIC

EAST ASIA AND THE PACIFIC

1. OVERVIEW

Entities from East Asia and the Pacific were the most active collectors of U.S. technology for the sixth consecutive year. In fiscal year 2009 (FY09), suspicious contact reports (SCRs) with an East Asian and Pacific nexus represented 36 percent of all such reports to the Defense Security Service (DSS), more than the next two leading regions combined.

Collectors from the East Asian and Pacific region continued to rely primarily on commercial companies to acquire sensitive U.S. technology and preferred to directly request sensitive technology from cleared contractor facilities. These suspicious entities continued to target information systems, sensors, and electronics technologies to augment their military modernization plans. Industry reporting in FY09 once again illustrated the region's willingness to acquire U.S. technologies through illegal means.

2. COLLECTOR AFFILIATIONS

In FY09, over half of the East Asian and Pacific-originated suspicious contacts stemmed from commercial entities. Entities with unknown affiliations, consisting mostly of those employing cyber collection techniques, were responsible for 17 percent of collection attempts, and government associated entities rounded out the top three collector affiliations with 15 percent of the reported collection attempts linked to this region.

Commercial collectors from this region used various avenues in attempts to acquire U.S. technology including: using U.S. government licensing

FIGURE 6

COLLECTOR AFFILIATIONS

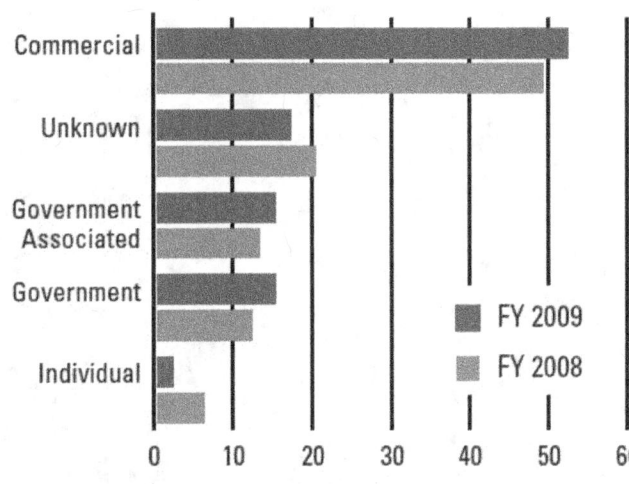

channels, using U.S. companies as intermediaries, and directly requesting to purchase goods.

East Asian and Pacific collectors continued to exploit U.S. universities and government-sponsored research institutes to acquire U.S. technology.[2, 3] In most of these incidents, graduate and post-graduate students from this region attempted to gain access to sensitive U.S. research and development (R&D) facilities through requests for visiting scholar research positions. Often, the solicitations for research positions were in military or sensitive dual-use technology areas. Students from the East Asian and Pacific region also contacted experts at cleared contractor facilities to request evaluations of technical papers.

Analyst Comment: Requesting U.S. technical experts to evaluate academic papers provides collectors an efficient, cost-saving exploitation method to both build rapport with experts and assists in determining which R&D paths hold promise and which are dead ends. Collectors likely use these papers as an opportunity to garner otherwise restricted information. (Confidence Level: High)

3. METHODS OF OPERATION

As in previous years, the direct request for information method of operation (MO) was the most common MO during FY09. East Asian and Pacific collectors employed this MO

FIGURE 7

METHODS OF OPERATION

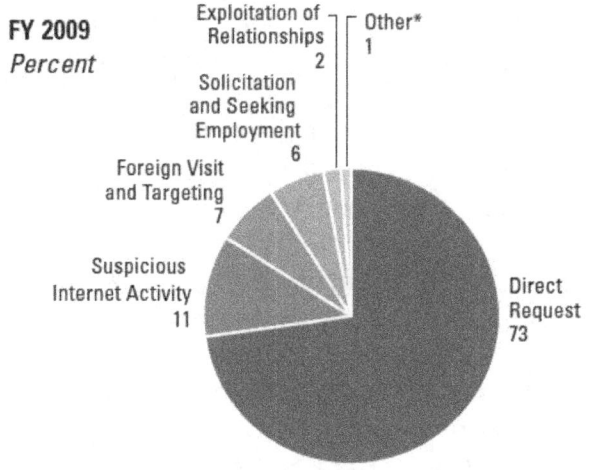

FY 2009
Percent

Exploitation of Relationships 2
Other* 1
Solicitation and Seeking Employment 6
Foreign Visit and Targeting 7
Suspicious Internet Activity 11
Direct Request 73

* Includes foreign employees and potential espionage indicators

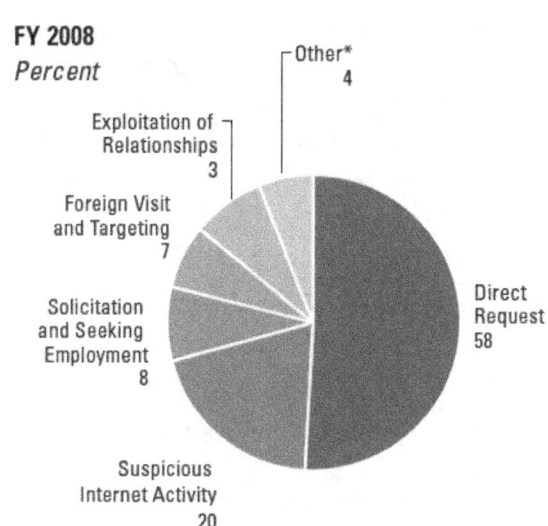

FY 2008
Percent

Other* 4
Exploitation of Relationships 3
Foreign Visit and Targeting 7
Solicitation and Seeking Employment 8
Suspicious Internet Activity 20
Direct Request 58

nearly 75 percent of the time when illicitly contacting cleared industry. These direct requests usually came in the form of an email to cleared contractors requesting to purchase specific products.

Not to be overlooked, suspicious Internet activity accounted for 11 percent of East Asian and Pacific-related SCRs in FY09, down from previous years' reporting but still representing the region's second most prolific collection MO. Although DSS noted a nominal decrease in the reporting of such incidents affiliated with entities in the East Asian and Pacific region, they were still more active in cyber operations than entities from any other region, accounting for more than half of all cyber-related SCRs received from cleared industry.

> *East Asian and Pacific collectors will continue to exploit the Internet to contact cleared industry directly while simultaneously pursuing cyber operations.*

Analyst Comment: The decline in overt FY09 cyber operations is likely more indicative of regional collectors increasingly finding ways to disguise suspicious Internet activity, rather than representing an actual decrease in cyber activity. (Confidence Level: Moderate)

4. TARGETED TECHNOLOGIES

Over the past year, East Asian and Pacific collectors most frequently targeted cleared industry for information systems, sensors, and electronics technologies.

Requests for information systems technology accounted for more than 20 percent of East Asia and Pacific-originated SCRs in FY09. Suspicious contacts related to aeronautics, last year's second-most commonly sought technology, decreased to only eight percent of reporting, trailing sensors and electronics technologies in this region.

Collection interest in sensors technology rose over the course of the past year, almost tripling in volume to encompass 17 percent of FY09 reports. Requests for sensors specifically included restricted technology related to radar, sonar, hyper-spectral imagery, and infrared imagery.

Analyst Comment: Although sensors technology supplanted aeronautics in the hierarchy of frequently targeted technologies, it is highly likely this decline was more attributable to increased sensors and electronics targeting, especially related to marine systems, as opposed to any real decrease in aeronautics targeting. As regional military forces engage in modernization campaigns, they will likely continue to actively target cleared industry to address current intelligence, surveillance, and reconnaissance limitations. (Confidence Level: High)

Electronics technology also saw a large increase in collection attempts, accounting for 11 percent of reported attempts from to the region. Most notably, suspicious entities sought technology related to radio frequency receivers, wave guides, and phase shifters.

Analyst Comment: The targeting of technologies associated with electronic warfare (EW) and those technologies that allow for secure command, control, communications, computer, intelligence, surveillance, and reconnaissance (C4ISR) systems is likely to continue. Cleared industry reporting confirms U.S. Intelligence

TABLE 1

TARGETED TECHNOLOGIES

Developing Science and Technologies List (DSTL) Codes	FY 2009 Percent	Developing Science and Technologies List (DSTL) Codes	FY 2008 Percent
Information Systems	21	Information Systems	24
Sensors	17	Aeronautics	11
Unknown	13	Unknown	10
Electronics	11	Marine Systems	10
Aeronautics	8	Positioning, Navigation, and Time	10
Positioning, Navigation, and Time	5	Laser and Optics	7
Armaments and Energetic Materials	5	Sensors	7
Marine Systems	4	Electronics	6
Ground Systems	3	Armaments and Energetic Materials	4
Laser and Optics	3	Materials and Processing	3
Space Systems	3	Space Systems	2
Materials and Processing	2	Ground Systems	2
Weapons Effects	2	Manufacturing and Fabrication	2
Biological	1	Chemical	< 1
Chemical	1	Energy Systems	< 1
Manufacturing and Fabrication	< 1	Nuclear	< 1
Energy Systems	< 1	Weapons Effects	< 1
Nuclear	< 1	Directed and Kinetic Energy	< 1
Signature Control	< 1	Signature Control	< 1
Biomedical	< 1	Biological	0
Directed and Kinetic Energy	0	Biomedical	0

Community assessments that EW is an increasingly important component of military modernization strategies within the region. It is also likely regional collectors will seek to augment reverse-engineering programs and aid indigenous EW and military efforts. (Confidence Level: Moderate)

5. ANALYTICAL FORECAST

It is highly likely East Asian and Pacific-based collection efforts will continue to use direct requests via commercial companies to acquire U.S. technology in the coming years. In addition, collectors will continue to exploit the Internet to contact cleared industry directly while simultaneously pursuing cyber operations. Entities from the East Asian and Pacific region will also likely try to establish new academic partnerships and exploit newly formed business relationships in an effort to acquire U.S. export-controlled or classified technology.

Considering efforts to push forward with military modernization plans, collectors will likely continue to target information systems and C4ISR

technologies resident in cleared industry to foster technical and military modernization programs. It is highly likely East Asian and Pacific entities will continue to circumvent traditional foreign military sales procedures and target information systems technology, including encryption devices, sensors, and electronics technologies related to EW and marine efforts, to satisfy their military modernization collection priorities. (Confidence Level: High)

CASE STUDY

Continuing a trend noted over the past three years, in FY09 cleared industry received multiple unsolicited email requests from universities and businesses in the region seeking autonomous underwater vehicles (AUVs).

In early spring 2009, two different AUV-producing cleared contractor facilities received separate, yet similar, emails from representatives of an East Asian and Pacific university specifically requesting AUV technology. DSS analysis linked the university to multiple illicit attempts to procure U.S. technology with military applications.

Following the initial solicitation, one of the cleared contractor employees received a second, similarly focused request from a commercial company in the region. This time, the suspicious individual requested a complete AUV. Several months later, the cleared contractor facility received additional requests for AUVs from an academic institution and another company, using the same method.

Analyst Comment: Industry reporting previously implicated the same university in specific efforts to acquire military information systems technologies. Analysis also linked the university to a foreign entity engaging in similarly focused collection activities. The considerable interest in AUV technology is likely attributable to a desire to improve tactical intelligence, surveillance, and reconnaissance capabilities for underwater operations. (Confidence Level: High)

This page intentionally left blank.

NEAR EAST

NEAR EAST

1. OVERVIEW

While collection activity associated with actors in the East Asian and Pacific region continued to dominate fiscal year 2009 (FY09) reporting, actors from the second most active region, the Near East, accounted for an increasingly significant share of suspicious incident reporting to the Defense Security Service (DSS). Although DSS noted some shifts in emphasis and technique, the type, manner, and focus of Near East collection efforts remained relatively consistent with the previous year's reporting.

FIGURE 8

COLLECTOR AFFILIATIONS

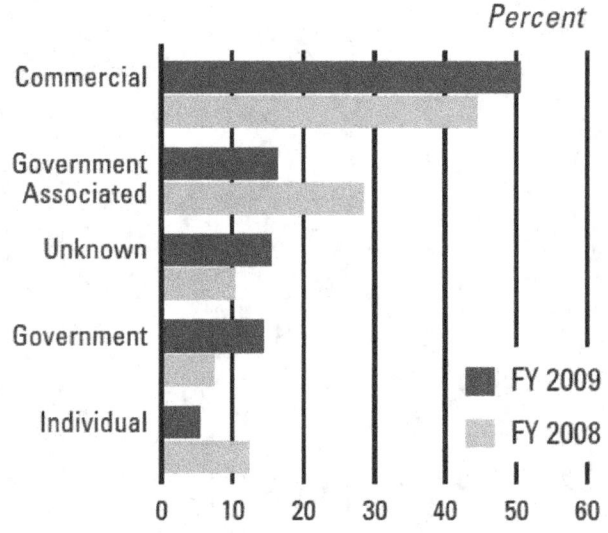

In FY09, Near Eastern collectors continued to focus their efforts on information systems, aeronautics, and sensors technology, primarily using direct requests as the preferred method of operation (MO). Solicitation and seeking employment once again represented the second most common collection method for Near Eastern actors, while exploitation of foreign travel and visits rebounded from a precipitous drop noted in FY08. Although only representing the third most commonly noted Near Eastern MO, this method witnessed the largest increase in FY09.

Not to be overlooked, Near Eastern entities continued to use a multi-faceted approach to target cleared industry, employing a wide variety of collection affiliations to include government-associated, commercial, and non-traditional collectors like students, professors, and engineers to mask true end-user affiliation.

2. COLLECTOR AFFILIATIONS

Similar to last year's findings, the commercial sector was, once again, the most prolific Near Eastern collector affiliation, accounting for half of all suspicious collection attempts targeting cleared industry. Near Eastern entities continued to use seemingly legitimate companies in apparent attempts to obtain classified technology or information, often routing requests through third parties in their efforts to circumvent export embargoes and trade sanctions.

The most dramatic change in regional collection attempts in FY09 was the increase of reporting on entities with unknown affiliations. These unknown entities were responsible for 15 percent of all collection attempts from the Near East, more than double the rate from the previous year.

Analyst Comment: Suspicious entities contacting cleared industry are providing less identifying

> *Near Eastern entities continued to use seemingly legitimate companies in apparent attempts to obtain classified technology or information, often routing requests through third parties.*

information and becoming more evasive likely in efforts to conceal any association with specific end-users, accounting for the increase in the unknown collector affiliations. Many of these masked collection activities were aided through the relative anonymity the Internet provides as a low-cost, high gain method to contact cleared industry. Cleared contractors should continue to be aware of this masked affiliation technique that shows no signs of future abatement. (Confidence Level: High)

FIGURE 9

METHODS OF OPERATION

FY 2009
Percent

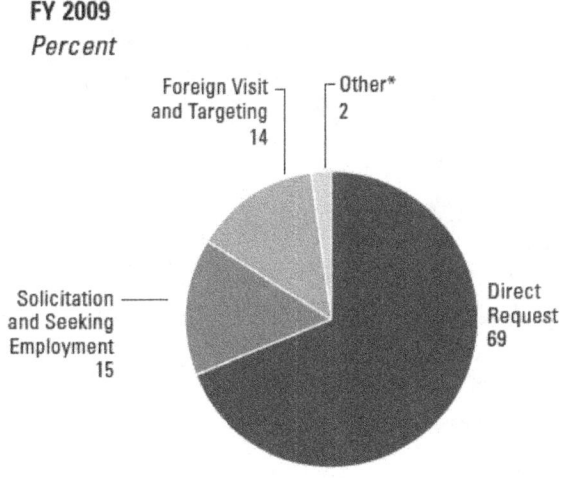

- Foreign Visit and Targeting 14
- Other* 2
- Solicitation and Seeking Employment 15
- Direct Request 69

FY 2008
Percent

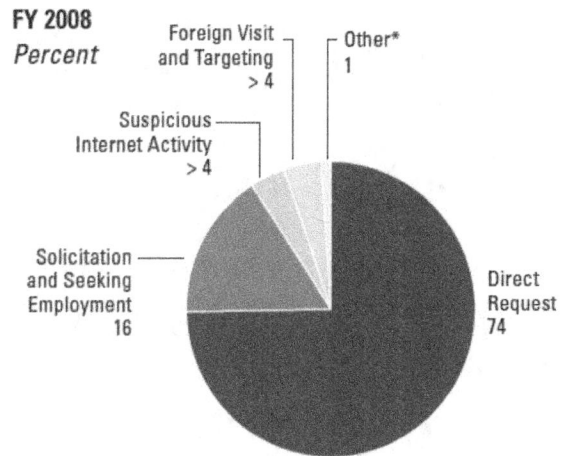

- Foreign Visit and Targeting > 4
- Other* 1
- Suspicious Internet Activity > 4
- Solicitation and Seeking Employment 16
- Direct Request 74

TABLE 2

TARGETED TECHNOLOGIES

Developing Science and Technologies List (DSTL) Codes	FY 2009 Percent	Developing Science and Technologies List (DSTL) Codes	FY 2008 Percent
Information Systems	20	Information System	28
Aeronautics	19	Laser and Optics	>23
Sensors	12	Aeronautics	15
Laser and Optics	8	Sensors	7
Electronics	8	Electronics	>5
Positioning, Navigation, and Time	7	Positioning, Navigation, and Time	>4
Marine Systems	5	Marine Systems	3
Unknown	5	Energy Systems	2
Ground Systems	4	Armaments and Energetic Materials	2
Armaments and Energetic Materials	3	Directed and Kinetic Energy	2
Materials and Processing	3	Chemical	1
Energy Systems	2	Biological	1
Chemical	2	Ground Systems	1
Space Systems	2	Manufacturing and Fabrication	1
Biological	1	Signature Control	1
Manufacturing and Fabrication	1	Nuclear	1
Weapons Effects	1	Materials and Processing	1
Directed and Kinetic Energy	0	Biomedical	0
Signature Control	0	Space Systems	0
Nuclear	0	Weapons Effects	0
Biomedical	0	Unknown	0

3. METHODS OF OPERATION

The most noteworthy change in this year's reporting was the apparent propensity of Near Eastern collectors attempting to exploit foreign visits and joint ventures to target and collect classified or restricted technology and information. Reports of Near Eastern actors using this method to contact cleared industry more than tripled from previous years, growing from four percent of all efforts in FY08 to 14 percent in FY09.

However, as has traditionally been the case, the direct request for information MO retained its position as the dominate collection technique, with Near Eastern collectors most frequently attempting to elicit information through emails, web-card submissions, faxes, phone calls, and face-to-face encounters.

Analyst Comment: Targeting using direct requests increases the number of targets of opportunity and likely increases the success rate for illegally acquiring classified or restricted U.S. technology. It is highly likely collectors commonly exploited this technique to pursue service agreements, joint ventures, or business relationships with U.S. cleared contractors in hopes of acquiring access to U.S. facilities, personnel, or classified technology. Once successful with the direct request method, Near Eastern collectors will often follow this approach with requests to visit sites within the United States seeking information outside standard official agreements. This strategy not only gains access to cleared industry but also increases opportunities to circumvent export control laws or sanctions. (Confidence Level: Moderate)

Although markedly less common than the use of direct requests, Near Eastern entities made consistent use of the solicitation and seeking employment method to acquire access, making that category the second-most common Near Eastern MO, replicating last year's placement. Several Near Eastern countries used non-traditional collectors such as university students, scientists, professors, and engineers as collection surrogates. These collectors approached cleared industry seeking research positions and student placement within various U.S. universities and research and development facilities.

4. TARGETED TECHNOLOGIES

Near Eastern entities continued to target information systems technologies with the same emphasis as evidenced in FY08. Entities from the Near East specifically targeted information systems related to U.S. sensor-to-shooter command, control, communications, computers, intelligence, surveillance, and reconnaissance (C4ISR) technology and aeronautics technology related to unmanned aerial vehicles (UAVs).

The most significant change in Near Eastern collection priorities during this reporting period was the decline of laser and optics targeting with a concomitant increase in illicit efforts to obtain sensors technology. Targeting of lasers and optics technology dropped from second to fourth place in the hierarchy directly behind foreign collection efforts for sensors technology.

Analyst Comment: Industry reporting demonstrated consistent targeting of laser and optics technology over the last few years. However, during this reporting period, collectors from the Near East likely augmented their targeting efforts by expanding collection to include sensors and electronics technology related to missile defense radars; anti-ballistic missile defense capabilities; and advanced intelligence, surveillance, and reconnaissance technology. This intense interest in missile defense technology is likely attributable to gaps in regional military defense technology and constant military modernization efforts. (Confidence Level: Moderate)

5. ANALYTICAL FORECAST

Near East collection efforts against information systems technology are likely to continue as the region attempts to acquire training simulators, software, and more sophisticated missile guidance and navigation technology necessary for force modernization. Advanced sensor systems, especially anti-ballistic missile radar systems, UAV control and weapons delivery technologies, and advanced C4ISR capabilities are likely to remain the focus of Near Eastern technology collection efforts. It is also likely

regional stability will continue to influence the type and intensity of regional collection priorities with a focus on dual-use technologies and early warning systems.

It is also highly likely Near Eastern collectors will continue to exploit the direct request MO in efforts to acquire classified or restricted U.S. technology and information. These regional collectors will continue to manipulate the Internet, as it offers a low-cost, high gain method to approach cleared industry either directly or through computer network operations.

Technology diversion through third-party nations and the use of front companies are likely to persist as embargoes and sanctions continue to impede Near Eastern opportunities to legally obtain U.S. technology. The exploitation of classified or restricted information and knowledge through academic exchange is also expected to continue. Furthermore, because of current embargoes on countries within the region and their aging military equipment, foreign efforts to illegally acquire U.S. technology are likely to persist. (Confidence Level: High)

CASE STUDY

The following example highlights a Near East technology collection attempt for export-controlled optical software through the use of students and professors to circumvent trade sanctions.

In FY09, an individual from the Near East contacted a cleared contractor facility using the company's online web form to request a demonstration and price quote for the optical software. The individual claimed association with a Near Eastern university.

DSS research revealed the requesting individual had previously contacted a cleared contractor employee seeking information and guidance on anti-satellite lasers. In this case, the individual stated he was studying optic and laser engineering.

Analyst Comment: Over the past several years, industry reporting has revealed significant Near Eastern interest in optical software, as it may be used in missile guidance systems. If Near Eastern collectors were successful in procuring the optical software it would likely allow them to reverse engineer and illegally obtain classified or restricted missile guidance technology.

Furthermore, Near Eastern collectors tend to favor the use of students and professors to obtain export-controlled U.S. information and technology. These non-traditional collectors not only offer foreign governments a seemingly legitimate way to contact cleared industry, but also allow a method to mask end-user affiliation. It is likely Near Eastern entities will continue using professors and students to target industry for classified or restricted technology and information. (Confidence Level: Moderate)

This page intentionally left blank.

SOUTH
AND CENTRAL ASIA

SOUTH AND CENTRAL ASIA

1. OVERVIEW

Based on cleared industry reporting for fiscal year 2009 (FY09), entities originating in the South and Central Asian region ranked as the third most prolific regional collectors of U.S. technology and information. Cleared contractor reports detailing South and Central Asian illicit attempts to acquire classified or restricted information and technologies nearly doubled from the previous year, totaling 15 percent of all reports received from cleared industry. The lack of vital equipment needed to support strategic and tactical objectives, aging military equipment, and a heavy reliance on foreign nations for repairs and maintenance of current weapons systems have all likely contributed to the increase in reported attempts by South and Central Asian entities to acquire sophisticated weapons and technology.

Consistent with the other regions, the majority of South and Central Asian collection efforts in FY09 used the direct request method of operation (MO). Direct requests accounted for 82 percent of all suspicious incidents in FY09 and primarily targeted sensors and electronics technologies. In addition to using commercial affiliates, foreign collectors from this region often used non-traditional intermediary agents, such as professors and students, to obtain classified or restricted information and technologies.

FIGURE 10

COLLECTOR AFFILIATIONS

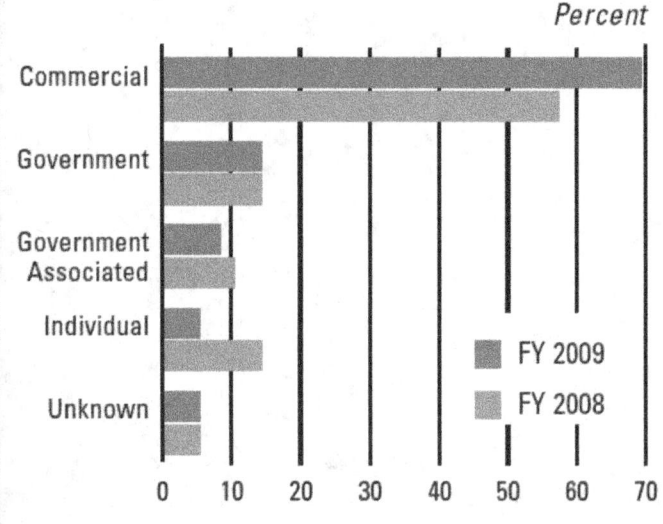

2. COLLECTOR AFFILIATIONS

Almost 70 percent of suspected South and Central Asian collection attempts in FY09 originated from the commercial sector. Continuing this dominating trend from the previous year, commercial collectors more than doubled their collection attempts, making it the most prolific collector affiliation for suspicious contact reports linked to this region.

While the collection attempts that DSS analysis directly linked to government officials or government associated entities rose slightly in FY09, the collection attempts involving entities from those two categories did not displace the sheer volume of contacts from commercial affiliates. Not to be overlooked, student collectors from the region were also active in seeking internship opportunities with cleared contractors.

Analyst Comment: The dominant commercial collection attempts from South and Central Asia will likely continue to be an ongoing trend. The expanding and increasingly integrated global business markets within the region *have allowed foreign collectors to shift from traditional government or military entities to commercial actors. Commercialization and privatization of some formerly government-directed businesses likely enhances this affiliation shift. (Confidence Level: Moderate)*

> *Governments within South and Central Asia are hoping to significantly improve their conventional military forces and approach some level of parity with neighboring regions' capabilities.*

3. METHODS OF OPERATION

Direct requests for cleared contractor information or technology comprised more than 80 percent of all South and Central Asian solicitations for U.S. technologies and information, making the direct request technique, by far, the most common method of operation

FIGURE 11

METHODS OF OPERATION

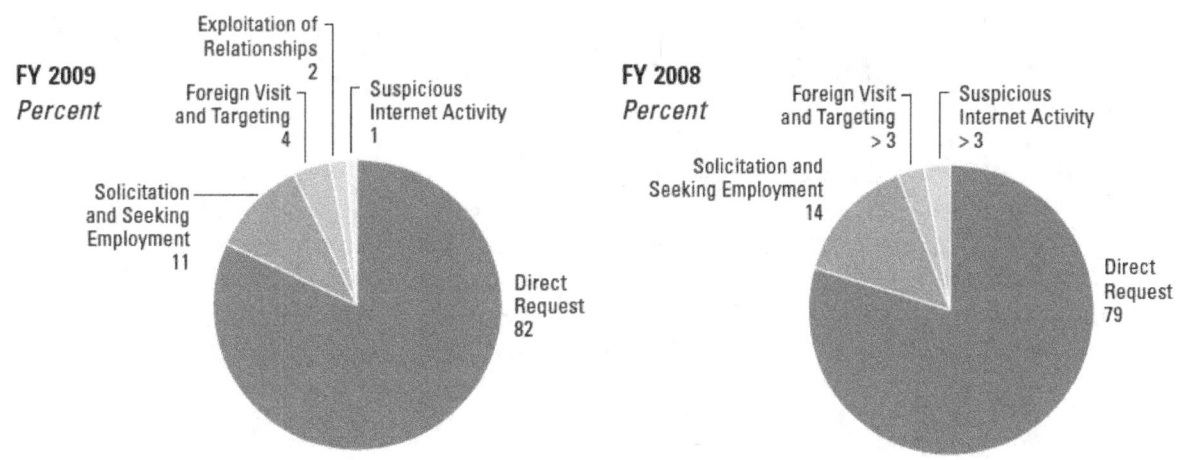

FY 2009 *Percent*

Exploitation of Relationships 2
Foreign Visit and Targeting 4
Suspicious Internet Activity 1
Solicitation and Seeking Employment 11
Direct Request 82

FY 2008 *Percent*

Foreign Visit and Targeting > 3
Suspicious Internet Activity > 3
Solicitation and Seeking Employment 14
Direct Request 79

TABLE 3

TARGETED TECHNOLOGIES

Developing Science and Technologies List (DSTL) Codes	FY 2009 Percent	Developing Science and Technologies List (DSTL) Codes	FY 2008 Percent
Sensors	19	Aeronautics	38
Electronics	17	Information Systems	24
Information Systems	14	Sensors	16
Aeronautics	13	Space Systems	5
Laser and Optics	8	Marine Systems	5
Positioning, Navigation, and Time	7	Positioning, Navigation, and Time	> 3
Armaments and Energetic Materials	4	Armaments and Energetic Materials	> 3
Marine Systems	3	Electronics	> 3
Biological	3	Laser and Optics	2
Ground Systems	3	Biological	0
Chemical	2	Biomedical	0
Energy Systems	2	Chemical	0
Materials and Processing	2	Directed and Kinetic Energy	0
Signature Control	2	Energy Systems	0
Unknown	2	Ground Systems	0
Space Systems	1	Manufacturing and Fabrication	0
Biomedical	0	Materials and Processing	0
Directed and Kinetic Energy	0	Nuclear	0
Manufacturing and Fabrication	0	Signature Control	0
Nuclear	0	Weapons Effects	0
Weapons Effects	0	Unknown	0

in FY09. Regional entities consistently used emails, web-card submissions, telephone calls, or facsimiles to request information and pricing in attempts to acquire classified and export-controlled U.S. technology.

South and Central Asian collectors also made significant use of the solicitation and seeking employment technique as a secondary means of acquiring information, with this method reflected in 11 percent of all reporting. These percentages have remained relatively consistent in recent years.

Analyst Comment: As the spread of technology through the integration of the global marketplace continues, the expansion of the international economy through trade and foreign direct investments will only increase foreign collection of U.S. technology. The continued growth of the information era and explosion of the digital age offer the ability to transfer information freely and provide instant access, likely promoting a more direct approach and effortless communication with cleared industry. (Confidence Level: High)

In FY09, industry reporting also indicated the increased use of U.S.-based South and Central Asian distributors as another avenue to potentially acquire controlled U.S. technology. Multiple FY09 requests originated from U.S.-based businesses whose owners appeared to be naturalized U.S. citizens. In these cases, DSS analysis attributed the suspicious requests to regional governments.

Analyst Comment: FY09 reporting indicated a slight change in regional collection tactics to obtain classified or restricted U.S. technology. U.S. citizens, acting as procurement agents on behalf of foreign governments, may contact cleared industry attempting to circumvent export control laws and restrictions. (Confidence Level: Moderate)

4. TARGETED TECHNOLOGIES

Based on FY09 reporting, South and Central Asian collectors expressed the most interest in technologies associated with sensors, electronics, information systems, and aeronautics technologies. Together, these four technology groups represented more than half of all the South and Central Asian collection efforts.

In FY09, regional entities focused primarily on sensors technology with emphasis on thermal imagers, night vision, surveillance systems, and various components related to radar systems. Requests for technical information related to electronics technology also increased in FY09, making it the second most sought-after technology category.

South and Central Asian collectors continued to target aeronautics in FY09, especially unmanned aerial vehicles. However, the volume of targeting focused on sensors and electronics technology and aeronautics dropped in the targeted technologies hierarchy from first position in FY08 to fourth position this year. During this reporting period, many of the sub-categories previously associated with aeronautics were targeted under sensors and electronics technologies, particularly intelligence, surveillance, and reconnaissance (ISR) platforms.

Analyst Comment: The top targeted technologies reveal the region's desire to improve remote sensor technology and field more capable ISR platforms. Governments within the region are hoping to significantly improve their conventional military forces and approach some level of parity with neighboring regions' capabilities. (Confidence Level: Moderate)

5. ANALYTICAL FORECAST

South and Central Asian entities will likely continue to target all aspects of export-controlled and classified U.S. technology with special emphasis on those technologies that promote the development of air, land, and sea-based defense capabilities and military sustainment. These collectors will also likely continue to use direct request methods of collection through email and the Internet as they offer low-cost, high gain opportunities to acquire classified or restricted technology.

Countries within the region will likely continue attempting to aggressively collect U.S. technology, with the ultimate goal of modernizing aging military equipment and deterring perceived threats from adversaries within and around the region. Regional governments will likely rely on foreign acquisitions and technology transfer agreements to modernize their militaries because they lack effective and innovative indigenous research and development programs. Concomitantly, these gaps may lead foreign collectors to exploit third-country transfers to obtain classified or restricted technology. (Confidence Level: Moderate)

CASE STUDY

In 2009, an individual representing South and Central Asian commercial company requested information and assistance from a U.S. cleared contractor employee related to export-controlled, gimbal technology, an essential component of a missile guidance and navigation system.

DSS research revealed numerous industry and Intelligence Community (IC) reports detailing this foreign company s efforts to acquire export-controlled or restricted technology from U.S. cleared industry. IC reporting characterized this company as specializing in military defense services and noted the company was wholly owned and operated by a foreign ministry of defense.

Furthermore, IC reporting estimated 70 percent of the company's output was for military end-users, including providing the components for ballistic missile and nuclear submarine programs.

Analyst Comment: Had the foreign company gained access to gimbal technology, it is highly likely it would have used the U.S.-developed technology in its own indigenous missile-development program. This would have significantly shortened R&D timelines, while in turn, advancing their technological base. Furthermore, industry reporting continues to validate IC assessments that foreign collectors use commercial companies as conduits to illicitly acquire technology they are unable to independently produce or procure. (Confidence Level: High)

EUROPE
AND EURASIA

1. OVERVIEW

In fiscal year 2009 (FY09), entities from the European and Eurasian region ranked as the fourth most active collectors of export-controlled or classified technology and information. In contrast to a downward trend noted over the last five years, the number of suspicious contact reports associated with the region increased slightly in FY09, accounting for 15 percent of all reporting from industry. However, analysis indicates the recent increase in reporting is due in part to the uncharacteristically high volume of reporting concerning targeting of cleared contractors at trade shows and conventions in the United States and abroad.

Commercial actors were the top European and Eurasian collectors of U.S. technology in FY09. The wide-variety of commercial enterprises identified within this affiliation category depicts a continuing regional preference for using a variety of collectors to target cleared industry. European and Eurasian collectors typically used direct requests as the preferred collection method of operation (MO), a consistent trend among the other regions of origin. Not surprisingly, collection

FIGURE 12

COLLECTOR AFFILIATIONS

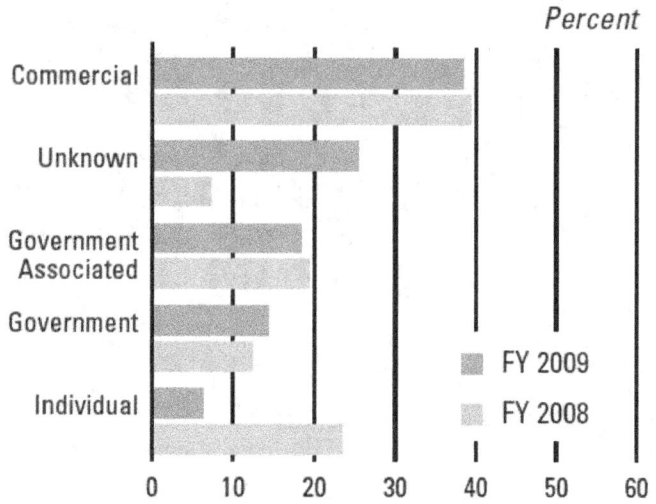

attempts remained focused primarily on aeronautics technology and specifically targeted unmanned aerial vehicle (UAV) systems.

2. COLLECTOR AFFILIATIONS

In FY09, commercial-affiliated collectors were responsible for nearly 40 percent of regional collection attempts targeting U.S. technology and information. The dominance of commercially-based inquiries represents a recurring trend noted over the past five years.

The most notable change in regional collector affiliations for FY09 was the dramatic increase in the number of collectors who successfully masked their affiliation, frequently using the Internet to remain anonymous. Collectors of unknown affiliation increased five-fold to become the second most prolific affiliation category, now representing 25 percent of all collection reporting associated with the region.

In contrast, the number of inquiries from individuals purportedly representing their own interests declined to six percent in FY09, down from 23 percent of collection attempts in FY08.

Analyst Comment: This surge in collection attempts of unknown affiliation is likely attributable to the anonymity the Internet offers. It is highly likely collectors will increase their use of the Internet as a low-risk, high gain approach for information, price quotes, or purchase requests to both directly contact cleared industry and obtain non-attributable network access to U.S. information and technologies. (Confidence Level: High)

Analysis indicates the recent increase in reporting is due in part to the uncharacteristically high volume of reporting concerning targeting of cleared contractors at trade shows and conventions in the United States and abroad.

3. METHODS OF OPERATION

Two commonly employed collection techniques, contacting cleared industry remotely and exploiting face-to-face contact to acquire information during foreign visits, accounted for an overwhelming 85 percent of all reported collection attempts attributable to European and Eurasian collectors in FY09.

Consistent with previous years' reporting, European and Eurasian collectors once again relied heavily on direct requests as the primary means to acquire information through the use of email, web-card submissions, phone calls, and in person requests for classified or restricted technology.

The most noteworthy change in FY09 was the increased exploitation of the foreign visits and targeting MO as a preferred collection technique. This MO accounted for 16 percent of all contacts, more than quadrupling the percentage reported in FY08. These foreign visits or targeting at trade shows and conventions allowed foreign entities access to cleared industry under the cover of commercial interest.

Analyst Comment: It is likely the increased use of foreign visits and targeting was related to a noteworthy increase in reporting from cleared contractor employees participating in trade shows and conventions. The proliferation of trade shows and conventions represent attractive targets of opportunity for aggressive technology collection. FY09 reporting reinforces historical collection trends suggesting that foreign collectors will continue to exploit these venues to target cleared industry. (Confidence Level: High)

4. TARGETED TECHNOLOGIES

Consistent with FY08 reporting, information related to aeronautics technology remained a European and Eurasian collection focus. Information systems, especially technologies associated with UAV ground station communications, was the second most targeted technology in FY09.

Based on industry reporting, the number of collection attempts directed against electronics and sensors technology doubled in FY09. Additionally, regional interest in armaments and energetic materials technology represented seven percent of reporting. In contrast,

FIGURE 13

METHODS OF OPERATION

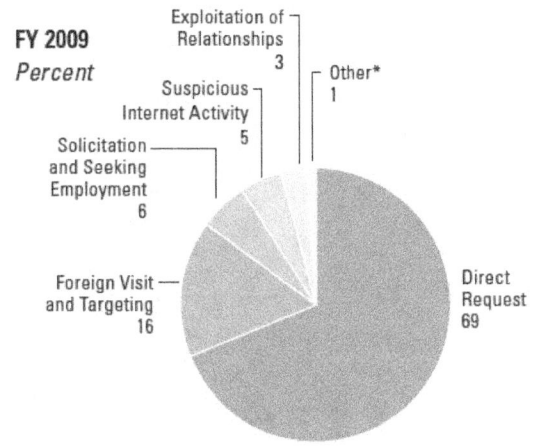

FY 2009
Percent

Exploitation of Relationships — 3
Other* — 1
Suspicious Internet Activity — 5
Solicitation and Seeking Employment — 6
Foreign Visit and Targeting — 16
Direct Request — 69

FY 2008
Percent

Foreign Visit and Targeting — 5
Other* — 4
Suspicious Internet Activity — 7
Solicitation and Seeking Employment — 11
Direct Request — 73

* Includes foreign employees and potential espionage indicators

EUROPE AND EURASIA

there were no reported collection attempts against this category in FY08. Entities originating from Europe and Eurasia likely targeted electronics, information systems, armaments and energetic materials, and aeronautics technologies to aid in the modernization of their indigenous armed forces and close technology gaps.

Analyst Comment: Based on requirements associated with regional military modernization

TABLE 4

TARGETED TECHNOLOGIES

Developing Science and Technologies List (DSTL) Codes	FY 2009 Percent	Developing Science and Technologies List (DSTL) Codes	FY 2008 Percent
Aeronautics	22	Aeronautics	30
Information Systems	16	Information Systems	12
Electronics	10	Laser and Optics	12
Sensors	10	Marine Systems	> 9
Laser and Optics	9	Electronics	7
Armaments and Energetic Materials	7	Sensors	7
Marine Systems	6	Materials and Processing	> 5
Unknown	6	Ground Systems Technology	> 5
Positioning, Navigation, and Time	5	Positioning, Navigation, and Time	3
Ground Systems	2	Weapons Effects	3
Nuclear	2	Manufacturing and Fabrication	1
Chemical	2	Nuclear	1
Materials and Processing	1	Energy Systems	1
Manufacturing and Fabrication	1	Space Systems	1
Space Systems	1	Unknown	1
Directed and Kinetic Energy	1	Armaments and Energetic Materials	0
Biological	0	Biological	0
Biomedical	0	Biomedical	0
Energy Systems	0	Chemical	0
Signature Control	0	Directed and Kinetic Energy	0
Weapons Effects	0	Signature Control	0

plans, targeting of aeronautics and missile system technology in cleared industry will not only likely continue, but will also likely facilitate regional efforts to upgrade defense systems and bolster indigenous research and development programs. (Confidence Level: High)

5. ANALYTICAL FORECAST

Indigenous requirements to modernize arsenals and enhance military capabilities continue to drive European and Eurasian actors to focus collection efforts on acquiring classified or restricted U.S. technology. Furthermore, it is highly likely European and Eurasian entities will continue to target cleared industry for aeronautics and information systems technologies, specifically to aid in the development of advanced indigenous UAV systems. Success in these collection areas will allow foreign entities from this region a more rapid and less expensive approach for indigenous research and development programs essential to modernization efforts.

It is likely entities within the region will attempt to exploit an increasing number of joint military operations with the United States to gain access and familiarity to cutting-edge, dual-use technologies. The rising number of corporate mergers and joint ventures involving Europe and Eurasia and the United States will likely fuel a continued desire for access to specific U.S. technologies. The access these venues afford will likely lower the profile of overt collection attempts, as governments seek to satisfy requirements through commercial surrogates without direct attribution. Targets of opportunity, such as trade shows and conventions, are likely to continue to present ample occasions for exploitation.

Clandestine methods effectively employed by some actors in the region likely mask the full range of collection activities targeting U.S. cleared industry. Similarly, the number of unknown-affiliated collectors will likely continue to increase as collectors continue to use the low-risk, high gain collection opportunities the Internet provides. (Confidence Level: Moderate)

CASE STUDY

While attending a trade show overseas, foreign entities targeted a cleared contractor employee. During a presentation on an aircraft system at the trade show, two individuals wearing press credentials demonstrated typical collection methodology. The two individuals videotaped the event, took abundant notes, and asked detailed questions in an attempt to elicit classified or restricted technology responses.

Later that evening, the same cleared contractor employee was with two colleagues when they noticed they were being followed to their hotel.

The following day, the same foreign collectors repeated their suspicious activities at several cleared contractor technology booths.

Analyst Comment: It is highly likely foreign intelligence entities will continue to demonstrate a willingness and capability to target and exploit cleared contractors at trade shows and exhibitions. (Confidence Level: High)

CONCLUSION

The volume and diversity of suspicious requests for information and technology from the cleared industrial base continued to increase in fiscal year 2009 (FY09). There was a nominal shift in overall hierarchy of regions of origin with the South and Central Asia and Europe and Eurasia in close competition for the third and fourth positions respectively. Although subtle, this change may indicate that collection activities in FY09 were more broad-based, with some traditional actors potentially masking affiliations by working through more innocuous surrogates.

Increased awareness and threat sensitivity from cleared industry is partially responsible for elevating the total volume and diversity of reports, including reports of collection attempts from non-traditional collectors, like students, who cleared industry may have previously considered purely innocuous.

According to industry reporting and analysis of suspicious collectors, East Asian and Pacific entities retained their status as the most prolific collector of U.S. technology with 36 percent of contacts originating from this region. Overt contacts in cleared industry with a nexus to this region more than doubled the volume from any other regional collector and dwarfed the suspicious collection attempts emanating from the second most active regional collector of U.S. technology, the Near East.

For the third consecutive year, the number of collection attempts identifiable with the commercial sector continued to grow, as those affiliated with the governmental sector declined as a percentage of the whole. This recurring trend likely indicates that foreign governments are increasingly dependent on commercial surrogates to collect and support national requirements instead of solely relying on state-sponsored entities. In addition, an increasingly globalized world market, facilitated by the ease of Internet connectivity, directly aids and fosters commercial collection attempts in cleared industry.

The exponential growth of the Internet and the difficulty of ascertaining the true origins of cyber-based inquiries frequently made it difficult to assess the requestor's definitive affiliation and, at times, the region of origin. As a result, the unknown affiliation category also increased in FY09 owing to instances where analysis could not directly attribute the contact to a specific end-user affiliation.

The method of simply asking for information or technology via the Internet, email, or telephone remained, by far, the most common technique used to acquire information from cleared industry, representing over 60 percent of all incidents. The dominance of the direct request technique has continued unabated since DSS began compiling statistics, underscoring the technique's apparent efficacy as a collection tool. However, collectors also used other methods to contact cleared industry such as exploiting foreign visits to cleared facilities, offering services, or soliciting business relationships in apparent attempts to acquire classified or restricted U.S. technologies.

Foreign entities continued to target information systems technology most frequently, primarily focusing on modeling and simulation software for military modernization programs.

In FY09 foreign collectors also employed the suspicious Internet activity method of operation, or cyber collection, in attempts to gain entry to cleared industry's networks and technology. Foreign entities routinely targeted cleared contractor networks in apparent attempts to penetrate computer systems and acquire data. East Asian and Pacific regional actors were particularly aggressive in conducting these cyber operations, representing over half of all such reported incidents.

Although the information systems category remained the most targeted, sensors technology, particularly radar and sonar, experienced the most dramatic increase rising from fourth place in last year's hierarchy of targeted technology to second in FY09. This increase was likely attributed to sensors technology as it relates to marine systems and programs. In particular, foreign entities targeted technologies identifiable with sonar buoys, autonomous underwater vehicles, and sensors for the Littoral Combat Ship program.

As DSS forecast in FY08, cleared industry reporting during this period indicated that foreign entities, primarily consisting of traditional rivals, emerging adversaries, and regional allies, continued to target the vast spectrum of cleared industry information and technologies for both commercial and military applications.

Access to cutting edge technology is an essential ingredient of competitiveness, whether that advantage is sought for political, military, or economic ends. Accordingly, classified or otherwise restricted information resident in cleared industry will remain the focus of international interest at all levels and attempts to acquire this technology through both legal and illegal means will only increase in the future.

As U.S. industry reaches out to foreign business partners to enhance its own economic competitiveness, access to sensitive technologies may become even more difficult to control. The combination of these two parallel dynamics will continue to fuel the unprecedented degree of interest in restricted or classified information and pose a challenge to balance the sometimes competing security and economic imperatives within the global marketplace.

Information systems technology (particularly command, control, communications, computers, intelligence, surveillance, and reconnaissance systems and modeling and simulation programs) and aeronautics will likely remain priority targets for industrially advanced countries involved in military modernization programs.

Other aeronautics-related technologies, such as unmanned aerial vehicle (UAV) systems, are also likely to remain foreign collection priorities. Countries with UAV research, development, and production programs will continue to focus on collecting information related to advanced UAV subsystems, while countries without indigenous UAV programs will seek complete UAV systems.

U.S. marine sensor technology will likely continue to be a target of Eastern and Central Asian navies as they advance into blue waters to protect their political and economic interests.

Sensors technology, especially radar sensor systems associated with missile defense technologies, will continue to be collection priorities for European and South and Central Asian entities while East Asian interests are expected to focus on sonar sensors. Established and emerging powers in these regions are likely to intensify efforts to acquire information related to missile guidance, positioning, and delivery systems.

It is likely that government and commercial collectors from both friendly and potentially adversarial nations will continue to seek advanced marine systems technology to bolster their naval modernization programs and develop or enhance their own arsenals.

Both state-sponsored and independent, non-governmental entities worldwide are expected to increase their cyber collection attempts against cleared industry. The continuous refinement of cyber reconnaissance competencies will allow foreign collectors to design even more efficient targeting plans employing the full range of collection techniques to acquire U.S. technologies of interest.

Foreign collectors will continue to seek the United States' dual-use technologies, irrespective of their commercial or military application. Acquiring such technologies enables foreign entities to advance their own technological research and development (R&D) capabilities and expand markets into technical fields otherwise beyond the scope or capabilities of indigenous R&D programs.

Foreign commercial and government entities will continue to exploit the gray areas of international business, blurring the lines between legitimate global business practices and illicit attempts to acquire U.S. technologies.

Foreign commercial and government entities will continue to exploit the gray areas of international business, blurring the lines between legitimate global business practices and illicit attempts to acquire U.S. technologies.

Rapid economic globalization will foster advanced technologies sales across borders where the end-user cannot always be determined, increased joint commercial endeavors with foreign firms, and accelerated foreign acquisition of U.S. companies involved with classified or restricted technologies. Although the majority of these efforts will be for legal and legitimate business purposes, hostile elements will orchestrate a portion of these foreign endeavors to gain access to sensitive U.S. technology for unauthorized transfer.

The inevitable dynamics of rapid globalization and increasingly competitive markets combine to create an environment where the integrity of U.S. classified information and technologies entrusted to cleared industry is at an elevated risk.

This complicated and challenging security environment demands that cleared contractor employees embrace their essential role as the "first line of defense" against those whose interests are inimical to U.S. interests. DSS security and counterintelligence professionals stand ready to assist cleared contractor employees in the critical defense of our nation's most sensitive technologies. (Confidence Level: High)

REFERENCE MAP

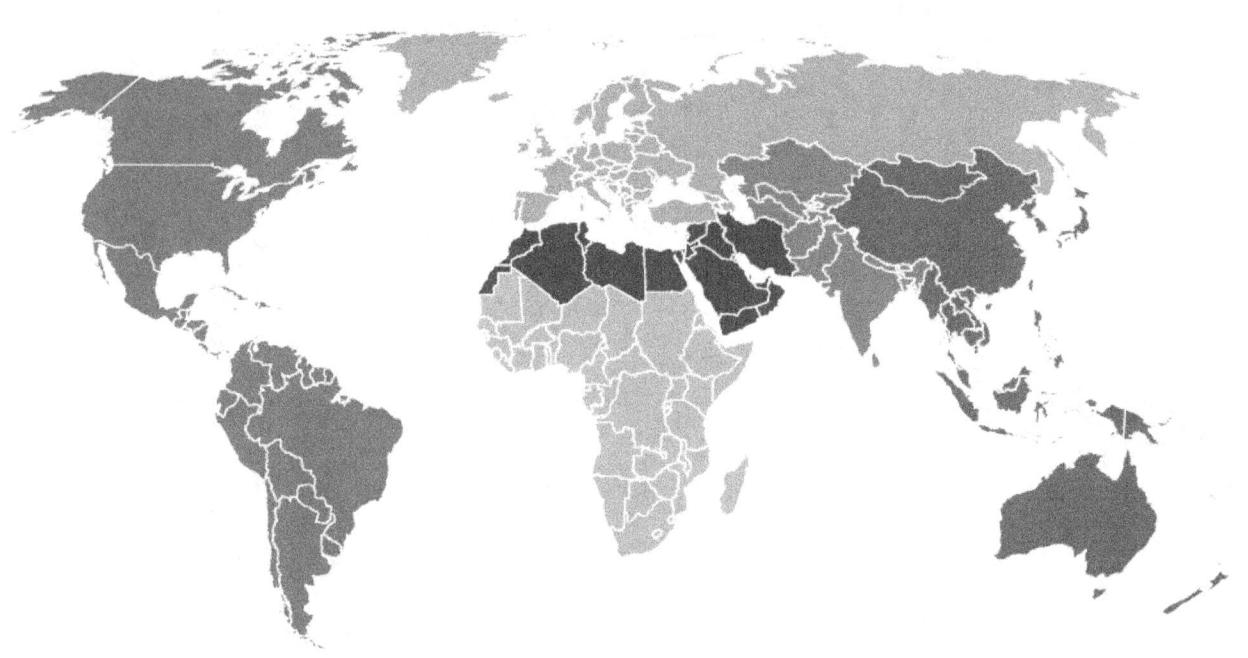

AFRICA	EAST ASIA AND THE PACIFIC	EUROPE AND EURASIA	NEAR EAST	SOUTH AND CENTRAL ASIA	WESTERN HEMISPHERE
Angola	Australia	Albania	Algeria	Afghanistan	Antigua and Barbuda
Benin	Brunei	Andorra	Bahrain	Bangladesh	Argentina
Botswana	Burma	Armenia	Egypt	Bhutan	Aruba
Burkina Faso	Cambodia	Austria	Iran	India	Bahamas, The
Burundi	China	Azerbaijan	Iraq	Kazakhstan	Barbados
Cameroon	Fiji	Belarus	Israel	Kyrgyz Republic	Belize
Cape Verde	Indonesia	Belgium	Jordan	Maldives	Bermuda
Central African Republic	Japan	Bosnia and Herzegovina	Kuwait	Nepal	Bolivia
Chad	Kiribati	Bulgaria	Lebanon	Pakistan	Brazil
Comoros	Korea, North	Croatia	Libya	Sri Lanka	Canada
Congo, Democratic Republic of the	Korea, South	Cyprus	Morocco	Tajikistan	Cayman Islands
Congo, Republic of the	Laos	Czech Republic	Oman	Turkmenistan	Chile
Cote d'Ivoire	Malaysia	Denmark	Palestinian Territories	Uzbekistan	Colombia
Djibouti	Marshall Islands	Estonia	Qatar		Costa Rica
Equatorial Guinea	Micronesia	European Union	Saudi Arabia		Cuba
Eritrea	Mongolia	Finland	Syria		Dominica
Ethiopia	Nauru	France	Tunisia		Dominican Republic
Gabon	New Zealand	Georgia	United Arab Emirates		Ecuador
Gambia, The	Palau	Germany	Yemen		El Salvador
Ghana	Papua New Guinea	Greece			Grenada
Guinea	Philippines	Greenland			Guatemala
Guinea-Bissau	Samoa	Holy See			Guyana
Kenya	Singapore	Hungary			Haiti
Lesotho	Solomon Islands	Iceland			Honduras
Liberia	Taiwan	Ireland			Jamaica
Madagascar	Thailand	Italy			Mexico
Malawi	Timor-Leste	Kosovo			Netherlands Antilles
Mali	Tonga	Latvia			Nicaragua
Mauritania	Tuvalu	Liechtenstein			Panama
Mauritius	Vanuatu	Lithuania			Paraguay
Mozambique	Vietnam	Luxembourg			Peru
Namibia		Macedonia			St. Kitts and Nevis
Niger		Malta			St. Lucia
Nigeria		Moldova			St. Vincent and the Grenadines
Rwanda		Monaco			Suriname
Sao Tome and Principe		Montenegro			Trinidad and Tobago
Senegal		Netherlands			United States
Seychelles		Norway			Uruguay
Sierra Leone		Poland			Venezuela
Somalia		Portugal			
South Africa		Romania			
Sudan		Russia			
Swaziland		San Marino			
Tanzania		Serbia			
Togo		Slovakia			
Uganda		Slovenia			
Zambia		Spain			
Zimbabwe		Sweden			
		Switzerland			
		Turkey			
		Ukraine			
		United Kingdom			

APPENDIX / REFERENCES

1 (U); Website; Diego Ruiz Palmer; NATO Review 2010; The End of the Naval Era?; www.nato.int/docu/review/2010/Maritime_Security/EN/; Ref 01 DEC 2010; (UNCLASSIFIED)

2 (U); Newspaper; Shelley Murphy and Marcella Bombardieri; the Boston Globe; FBI warns colleges of terror threat: Asks more vigilance on theft of research; 12 JUN 2007; www.boston.com/news/education/higher/articles/2007/06/12/fbi_warns_colleges_of_terror_threat/; Ref 01 DEC 2010; Investigative Journalism; (UNCLASSIFIED)

3 (U); Report; Office of the National Counterintelligence Executive; Annual Report to Congress on Foreign Economic Collection and Industrial Espionage, FY 2008; 23 JUL 2009; www.ncix.gov/publications/reports/fecie_all/fecie_2008/2008_FECIE_Blue.pdf; Ref 01 DEC 2010; Threat Assessment; (UNCLASSIFIED)